Table Of Contents

- Hot Air Balloons

- Weird 101

- Weird It All Begin?

- Your Dream Job Guaranteed!

- STAR POWER

- Weird Little Cupcakes (Marketing)

- Mic Drop

Chapter: Hot Air Balloons

Come to think of it, it was pretty random writing a short story about ice cream cones, while aboard a hot air balloon, hovering over Paris. But man-oh-man, the view was all kinds of magical!

If you thought for a second that my introduction was extremely weird and completely false... You're absolutely right. If however, my little imaginary adventure was true and that story became a New York Times Best Seller, every aspiring writer would be lined up waiting for the next hot air balloon to take them away into their anticipated writer's bliss. Weird is contagious. I've been the proud founder and retail magician of a multi-award winning tea company for over five years now, and I can shamelessly admit, that the majority of opportunities and success

I have been fortunate enough to experience, was usually on account of people thinking I was weird.

I know, weird right? When I think about the word weird and what... or should I say whom that might look like, none other than Waldo comes to mind. From a strategic marketing standpoint, the entire 'Where's Waldo' concept is straight up genius. A semi-geeky nomad, dressed in a red and white striped sweater and a matching toque, with a random walking cane, has kept people pondering for years. Where the heck is Waldo? The most important takeaway for any business, brand or aspiring entrepreneur is not just the characteristics of Waldo, but instead it's the "Where!"

Ask any PR professional and they'll explain to you how difficult it can be to get anybody to care about you or your business, let alone as much as ask questions like "who, what, where, when or how?" There is so much going on in the world of commerce, making it extra difficult to get peoples attention, but weird people like Waldo, keep us interested and entertained almost effortlessly.

There are so many benefits in being classified as "strange" or "different" or "odd" and I hope to shed some light on these weird little secrets that will help you, and your inquisitive and inspired mind to discover success in a new and adventurous way. Hey, who knows maybe one day you'll be as weird as Waldo!

Chapter: Weird 101

Hmmm. What's the best way to kick this entire topic off? I certainly don't think it's fair that we jump right into everything without first discussing what it means to be weird. Yes, I am targeting my perspective towards the businesses-startups, entrepreneurs and marketing enthusiasts alike, but technically speaking this book can be consumed by anybody. I heard an amazing quote in the past that said, "Weird people don't sit around wondering if they're weird." Isn't that the truth! Weird is not something that a person sits down and calculates and strategically plans. It's authentic, it's true, and it's natural. I've never self-proclaimed myself to be weird or different or unusual, as I feel that the moment someone can consciously say of themself, "I am weird." you immediately cease to be weird. Think of it like a person bragging to everyone about themselves saying, "I am humble." Actually, that's probably the most non-humble thing you could ever say. So therefore I restate my case, that weird is not something that's practiced or self proclaimed but rather pronounced by others. People tell me I'm crazy everyday because of the farfetched ways that I choose to promote my company on social media. Whether I'm dressed in a ragdoll costume doing summersaults in the shop or walking the main streets dressed as a gigantic lime wedge promoting my lime flavoured green tea, people think I'm weird, but they love it and most importantly, I love it.

What is it that they actually love? As handsome as I may think I am, I highly doubt that people are just in love with me. There's got to be something about what I'm doing that evokes some kind of appreciation in others. BINGO! I've got it: People naturally respect the things they are not willing to do themselves.

The Laws Of Appreciation

The simplest definition of appreciation is: The estimation of the qualities of something, for the sole purpose of properly valuing that thing or person. We as human beings naturally enjoy giving recognition to the things we find amusing, entertaining, skillful, and challenging. In and of ourselves, we know how difficult it can be to even attempt to try something that we're not one hundred percent confident about. A very common example would be public speaking. We can almost instantly recall a past scenario where we were put on the spot or placed in an uncomfortable situation where we had to speak in front of a group of people, and we're reminded of the instant sweat under the arms, the rapid heat that took over our entire body and the good ol' butterflies in the stomach feeling. Yes, these are feelings we don't easily forget. On the contrary, when we see someone else comfortably or confidently doing the same things we are nervous or afraid to do, we tend to express our appreciation for that person and their ability to do what we find so daunting, easily. Or on the other hand, you get straight up jealous.

Keeping things positive, it's the appreciation factor that I'd like to highlight here, because if we can effectively apply this kind of thinking to our jobs, careers or business ventures, we will certainly be able to attract more appreciators to our cause. Whether you are operating a startup, mom & popshop, medium sized business or large corporation, you will eventually have to spend what could be a healthy sum of money on marketing. Now I absolutely plan on digging in a little deeper into the topic of marketing as the book progresses, but now is a good time to mention that many businesses waste thousands of dollars on marketing efforts that simply get swept under the rug, mainly because they did not evoke any sense of emotion or appreciation from their intended audience. They leave the potential consumer thinking "WHO CARES!" Believe me, I am super-guilty of this kind of ineffective marketing as well. The worst kind of marketing campaign or advertisement is the one that the customer understands too much.

That's probably the weirdest thing you've ever heard. I know, but just swim with me for a second I'll explain. When a customer understands your marketing efforts too much, it means that what you're doing is too normal. Have you ever watched a movie, and you were able to figure out the entire plot, climax, twist and conclusion in the first five minutes? Two thumbs down right? It's the exact same thing in marketing. Customers and clients don't want to be able to figure out your next promo or marketing campaign with little to no effort, because that means you are robbing them of the mystery, the excitement, the anticipation and the weirdness. Yes, this is usually why a company will experience poor results when measuring their marketing metrics; their intended audience understands them too much.

<u>The Laws Of Understanding</u>

Anything that people don't understand is automatically classified as weird. Weird is just another word for unusual, abnormal or strange. But a fair question to ask would be; if something were abnormal to you, but normal to me, then is it fair to generally classify that thing as weird? I am well aware that a question of such nature could easily spark a debate that would last a century, but I'm responsible for cooking dinner tonight, so let's try to find middle ground. Our understanding is the only guide that we have when it comes to our evaluation of what is normal and what is abnormal. My entire high school math experience was abnormal to me because I didn't understand one thing that was taught. It was almost like another language. "Pie-R-Squared Equals 3.16 to the power of BEDMAS? WHAT?" Can I get an "F" for foreign language please? However, there were many students in my class who would skim over their math tests as if it were the 'ABC's. The only difference was that they understood it and I didn't.

Math itself is not weird or abnormal, my perception about math made it weird to me.

Great! Now with all that craziness behind us, it is now safe to say that people will only call you or what you do weird, because they don't understand you. As they open themselves up to understanding who you are and why you do what you do, you become less and less weird to them. Twenty years ago, if you saw someone walking down the street taking pictures of them self for no apparent reason, you would say "weird!" Fast forward to 2016, the word 'selfies' (which refers to a person taking pictures of them self) is actually popping up in our dictionaries! I mean, if you're NOT taking selfies, you're weird! It took time for society to understand this new behavior, but once understood it became the new standard. Weirdness is a very temporary evaluation of someone or something, because eventually people will gain a better understanding of that person or thing and embrace them as the new normal.

Well, I think I have pretty much dissected the basics of what weird actually is. Now it's time to discover the many ways we can actually apply all this weirdness to help build and or grow our businesses. Let's have some fun! "Wheeeeeeeeee!"

Chapter: Weird It All Begin?

Where in history did awkwardness and weird behavior become a tool that can be used to better market people and companies? Well, one can never be sure as to where and when this weird epidemic began, but there are a lot of companies and people in general who are experiencing a taste of success because of it.

Would you ever go out to shopping mall, purchase a really comfortable blanket and then go home and cut two armholes into that same blanket? Probably not right? Well, Snuggies (which originated from the primary concept called The Slanket) would beg to differ, because they did exactly that. I'm sure you would agree with me, that nothing screams cozy like a hot chocolate, Netflix and your favourite Snuggie on chilly night. Many skeptics rejected the idea of a wearable blanket, and even to this day if you take a look on review sites and online forums, you'll see that some people think the entire concept is straight up ridiculous. Yes, maybe it is. But the ridiculousness of the Snuggie/Slanket seems to be the main reason why they are in such high demand. After all, if you're weird enough to wear a Snuggie, you're cool enough to stand out.

Weird-itus, (a new word I just created to describe the syndrome of being weird) has also been discovered and practiced in the music industry. For years, music artists have searched for new ways to stay relevant, stand out and most importantly sell more records. Among some of the most popular music artists of all time, we find some of the strangest characteristics, weirdest personalities, abnormal songs and un-imaginable outfits, all in the name of weirdness. Let's debrief. First up, we have two French men who decided to blend their passion of electronic music and infuse it with their obsession with robots. Weird right? Well, after millions of records sold worldwide and with a shiny Grammy Award under their belt, electronic masterminds Daft Punk continues to astonish music lovers all over the globe. If that's enough, the weirdness gets even more elevated when you learn that to this day, Daft Punk refuses numerous interviews and live appearances and even when they do show up, they mysteriously hide behind their futuristic, robotic helmets. Agreed, strangely awesome.

Lady Gaga is nothing shy of the weirdest person on the planet when it comes to her taste in fashion. When I say taste, I mean literally. In 2010, Lady Gaga shocked the VMA's (Video Music Awards) when she walked the red carpet, dressed in raw beef, yes, raw beef. The dress was later referred to as, "The Meat Dress" and is now displayed very securely in The Rock Hall Of Fame. Let me guess… You're wondering about the condition of the dress today? Umm. Let's just say, it has now transformed into "The Beef Jerky Dress" Gross. This fashion stunt definitely caused a huge "beef" in the media, as it stirred up everyone from animal activist, to feminist, to vegan ambassadors and of course anti-fashion groups.

The purpose? No clue, maybe just a delicious controversy?

The result? Six Grammy Awards, including Album of the year. She won the 2010 Best International Album at The BRIT Awards. In 2013, Rolling Stone named her album titled *FAME* as one of the "100 Greatest Albums Of All Time." It's safe to say, she's probably thinking, wow! Success has never looked so yummy.

Great Daniel! So you're basically saying, "lets all skip over to our local meat shop, cut out a cool outfit and head to our next business meeting!" Well, no. But what I am saying is that weird concepts, and weird people, cause us to react. If you're in business and not focusing on causing some reaction to the content and material that you put out there...Then what are you really doing? Why waste your time designing a basic flyer, with basic images and a contact number and hoping that you're going to somehow cause some unexpected response and drive sales? It just doesn't add up. Normal efforts produce normal results. Extra-terrestrial efforts on the other hand, well, they produce results that are out of this world. (I am currently smiling in appreciation for my last witty comment.)

The title of this chapter is "Weird it all begin?" Although we weren't able to find a start date to this "weird-itus" epidemic, we can all agree that the weird trend has indeed started.

Chapter: Your Dream Job Guaranteed!

Ever dreamed about working for an amazing company that offers out of this world benefits and great pay? Welcome aboard to the "Rest Of The World" Ship! Everybody's looking to land that perfect job or career, (If they aren't already creating it themselves!) So... How do you go about grabbing the company's attention, impressing their HR department and getting that first interview? Simple! THROW YOUR RESUME IN THE GARBAGE RIGHT NOW!

Before I was the one doing the hiring, I use to be the person handing out resumes, and if I had known then what I know now, I would have had 100% success rate with at least getting to the interview stage! So, what's the trick? Brace yourselves; it's a weird one. Print your resume on a purple piece of paper! Ok fine. If your favourite colour is orange you can use that too.

Huh?

Yes! Print your resume on a bright purple or pink or yellow piece of paper! You're guaranteed to get an interview with the company you've always dreamed about working for. You're probably thinking... "What the heck is in this guy's tea?" I know it sounds crazy, but I'll explain. Every year I receive hundreds and hundreds of boring, repetitive and straight up 'blah' resumes with individuals that claim they want to "obtain a position within my company, to apply their skills blah blah blah blah blah!" and we are all guilty of handing out these wastes of paper. But seriously, they're lucky if they ever get a second glance. This truth brings me to my (proven) purple resume theory, which you are more than welcome to try. It has a 100% success rate. By printing your resume on a crazy, abnormal coloured piece of paper or with a weird, stand out design, only 1 of 2 things will happen:

1) The Employer Will Think...
What is that purple piece of paper sticking out like

a sore thumb in this pile of resumes? When they pull it out, lo and behold your awesome resume is now starring them in the face and peaking their interest and stirring their curiosity. Why would this person choose to display such a professional, definitive document in such a creative, different and crazy way? Hmmm..... What other magical characteristics does this person poses? I'd like to meet this person and see who they are and why they decided to be different. Maybe they can help our company to think different.

Congrats! You just landed interview number 1 because you challenged the creative capacity of the company! Well done.

On the other hand...

2) The Employer Will Think...
What is that purple piece of paper sticking out like a sore thumb in this pile of resumes? When they pull it out, lo and behold your annoying resume is now starring them in the face and aggravating

their professional image and standards. Why would this person choose to display such a professional, definitive document in such a silly, childish and ridiculous way? Just imagine the other sarcastic and unsophisticated schemes they're capable of! Definitely not the person we're looking for. Congrats! You didn't land the interview because you gave the company a heads up of your creativity and magical personality and they didn't like it! Well done! You just spared yourself years of misery, and unnecessary stress, working for a company where you have to hide your true character, abilities and ideas just to "fit the role."

Now wouldn't you rather work for a company who does accept the "purple resume?" (In other words accepts you as the person that you truly are?) If a company can see value in your ability to express your creative side, then this is a company where you can see yourself enjoying and growing and contributing to their success! Yes, this is your DREAM JOB!

In conclusion, do something absolutely out of this world with your next resume and you'll be surprised how quickly and effortlessly you filter out the "Jobs from hell," and land your DREAM JOB! I guarantee 100% success rate or your book reading time back! LOL. Good luck! Love Dan.

Chapter: STAR POWER

This chapter is kind of like my little "success story" rant. That's what makes a good read right? Well, I hope so. When it comes to my many inspirations and influences, I find that for some reason I tend to always gravitate to some cartoon, or animated character or movie personality to draw references. I don't know why, but it just seems to work for me. The famous mystery puzzle character 'Where's Waldo' is who inspired the title of this book, but everyone that has ever heard me speak knows that Super Mario is definitely one of my biggest inspirations! I just knew it! There's no possible way one of the most popular video games on earth, was simply about a tiny, Italian plumber with a thick mustache, who collects coins, beats up giant turtles hoping to save a princess named peach... I knew there had to be a deeper meaning to the magical world of Super Mario. One of my most requested keynote presentations today is "*How Super Mario Helped Me Grow My Business.*" This presentation walks the audience through my company's step-by-step growth strategy, using the characters from Super Mario to represent and teach us all very valuable lessons in business. Do you mind if I share one of these characters/ lessons with you? I'm sorry; I couldn't hear your answer so I'm going to take that as a yes!

Player 1 [Press Start.]

Star Power

Everyone knows the infamous super star in Mario and the powers it possesses. Mario is a normal little superhero with more work ethic than actual super powers. He has his ups and downs, moments when he is handing it to the evil mushrooms and times when he is hopeless. Suddenly Mario hits a random brick box and out comes the star! He immediately gets it and "KABOOOOM!," Mario officially transforms into this multi-coloured, glowing, superhuman who can break through walls, trample over his enemies and ward off any items being thrown at him. In other words, he is unstoppable!

During my start up years, I was that little normal man who everyday would work hard just trying to stay busy. I thought being busy meant being successful... Like many of us, we tend to naturally adapt to our surroundings, whether it be at work, in the office, at the mall, or in the local grocery store. Take for example that "happy-go-lucky" kind of person, who is always upbeat and living in the moment. Usually we don't let people see that side of us, unless we've known them for years and are comfortable around them. There's absolutely nothing wrong with suppressing our real personality, when we're in unfamiliar situations, but I came to realize that hiding who I really was when in public was actually working against me. The real me is where the star power was! I love to laugh, I love to perform, I truly enjoy dressing up in funky, weird outfits and costumes!

Ok, not Lady Gaga weird, but you know what I mean. I didn't think business allowed this kind personality. I decided to play it safe and be more reserved in business. It felt so unnatural, so 'not-like-me.' It was at that moment, I realized that I was no longer willing to shade who I really was inside just to appear "business-like" or "professional."

[Enter in STAR POWER]

That amazing person you display when you're with your best friend... That's Star Power! That hilarious uncle you can be at family gatherings... That's Star Power! That great listener, that talented singer, that always-matching Fashionista you are on the weekend... That's Star Power! Star power is simply the ability to unleash that unique quality inside of us, that makes us the special person that we truly are. In my opinion, if I have to hide that, just to fit in to my surroundings, I'd rather not be in that kind of surrounding. Success began to pour in the moment I began applying this kind of thinking. Does it sound kind of cheesy? Weird? Maybe, but it worked for me! What's your star power?

Chapter: Weird Little Cupcakes (Marketing)

I'm going to make the assumption that this is probably the most weird, yet delicious chapter title you've read all day...? Me too. I'd like to dedicate this chapter to all the marketing masterminds out there, or for those aspiring to be the same.

 Whether you are operating a multi-million dollar company or you just launched your first start up business, marketing is one of those things that cannot be ignored. If done right, you can experience substantial growth in all areas of your business, yes including the bottom line. However, when marketing is done poorly, it can literally mean the death of any business irrespective of the quality products or services you claim to offer.

So what does this mean to you, the reader?

Well, when you're drafting up your next marketing plan, you'd better make sure that thing is as good as a cupcake!

{Enter in yummy cupcake- stage 3}

Pardon my attention to detail; I thought the whole "enter in cupcake thingy" was quite cute... Apart from highlighting and offering tips about marketing in this chapter, my subconscious goal was also to demonstrate that it is very possible, in fact recommended, that you (the reader) find influences for your business venture or company, from some of the weirdest and most random concepts, people, places or objects, hence the cupcakes.

Without further a due, here are 3 major marketing lessons that you can learn from a cupcake... YES! A CUPCAKE! If you can gobble up this information and apply it to your business, I guarantee that you'll have people drooling over your delicious new ideas!

1) The Recipe

 Think about your favourite cupcake shop; now think about your favourite flavour. Drooling yet? Well, let's break down why you are so head over heels about that mouth watering delicacy.

It's certainly not your favourite cupcake because it tastes good... It's your favourite cupcake because it tastes good ALL THE TIME! The consistency of that cupcake is what keeps you coming back for more. On the baker's side of things, there's only one way to keep those cupcakes consistent. YOU GOT IT! THE RECIPE! Bridgette or Bob the baker at some point, figured out a recipe, a strategy, a formula that is so exact, so precise, tested-n-tasted, and as long as they stick to that recipe, they know what to expect with every batch of cupcakes that comes out the oven. Marketing/ branding is no different. Instead of winging your next promo, or randomly coming up with your next marketing campaign. It's better to evaluate what works for you in your business, what do your customers and clients rave about? What resonates with them? Are they more interactive when you produce emotional content? Humour? Information & facts? Learn what works and then tailor your recipe accordingly. If done successfully, it will no longer matter WHAT you do, but instead HOW you do what you do, and that is your secret recipe!

2) Cupcake? Or Muffin? WHAT ARE YOU!

One of the biggest marketing mistakes too many companies make, is trying to be everything to everyone. #FAIL. If you're a cupcake, be a cupcake, don't try to be a muffin too. Just incase you're wondering how this analogy actually makes any sense; please do allow me to explain. A Muffin can be so appropriate for so many periods during the day. You can have a muffin for breakfast, muffin for lunch, muffin after dinner, heck you can even have a muffin when you're sleeping! Ok, I went a bit over board... but the point I'm trying to make is that you can't really categorize a muffin in any specific way or for any specific time. On the flip side, you probably won't find many people having cupcakes for breakfast or lunch... (Wipes cupcake crumbs off my face at 8 A.M.) When you think of cupcakes, it's special, it's a treat, it's a dessert, it's a surprise, it's that little reward at the end of a long work day that we gift to ourselves or someone we care about. Your marketing should be the same. Instead of trying to be the perfect fit for every scenario, strategically set a target, master that target and be your customers/ clients little reward at the end of every day. This was the same thinking my wife and I applied to our teashop, hence the reason to this day we still do not sell coffee.

Another company who has done this very successfully is Crocs (the not so appealing-yet convenient foam slipper.) Instead of trying to tap into the sports footwear, luxury fashion and business footwear sector, they just make that darn foam slipper and they are EXTREMELY successful at it. What or who is your company's main marketing focus?

3) LOOK DELICIOUS!

Before you ever decided that you were deeply in love with that vanilla-strawberry, cream filled, cheesecake icing cupcake from your favourite local cupcake shop... You had to choose it based on how it looked. Yes, every cupcake must past the "oh-so-yummy **looking**" stage first, before it gets to the "yummy **tasting**" stage. Your marketing and company branding is no different. My golly-gosh, make it look delicious why don't you! Businesses get so caught up in all the ingredients and preparation that go into their company; that they completely forget that the final product is suppose to look yummy. I don't care how much of an expert you are in, [fill in your expertise] if your business card is ugly, then it's going in the garbage. No offence, but if your business card has a blank white backside, at most I may use it to write down an old friends phone number, or an account balance when I'm phone banking. People aren't trying to be disrespectful when they toss your business card or promotional flyer in the trashcan; it's just that it doesn't look good enough for them to keep it. Now, with that thinking in mind, imagine how potential clients feel about your website, your blog posts, your social media landing page, your menu, your flyers, your retail shop etc. The list goes on. Your goal in marketing is to be that mouthwatering cupcake that has a light shinning down on it as it patiently waits in that glass dessert case to be purchased, unraveled and gobbled in only 3 bites. Now that's what you call yummy marketing! I hope this in someway helps you define or re-define your marketing efforts or at the least, urges you to get over to your local cupcake shop and stuff your face! I'm out yo, peace!

Chapter: Mic Drop

When a music artist or speaker or pretty much anyone that uses a microphone, feels they have finished their job and "rocked the mic," they drop the mic. Pretty gangster right? Well, we have now come to the point in this book where I am dropping the mic. I have shared as much weird information as I can possibly think of at this moment, and hopefully nudged you enough to maybe change your approach to business. If there's one take home lesson here that we can all agree on, it's that everyone is weird in their own way. At some point in life, we have all been misunderstood or misinterpreted and looked at like we came from another planet. All I'm saying, is that the unidentifiable things about us, are in fact what make us unique, one of a kind, irreplaceable and interesting. You apply that weird little way of thinking to business, and you've got your self something really worth checking out.

If you made it this far, then I can safely assume that you enjoyed this read or maybe you were just really curious as to where I was going with this whole weird thing. Maybe the bus ride was just really long, or the flight was intensely boring. Maybe that coffee break was just a tad exaggerated and intentionally lengthened? Perhaps you're on a wild motivational adventure, seeking out some majestic inspiration! Whatever the case may be and whatever your reason is, you are now left with one single question; what do you do now? Do you fly to Paris, jump in a hot air balloon and write about ice cream cones? Do you head to the city library and search for a classic *'Where's Waldo'* book? Do you start ferociously plugging away at that long awaited business plan? Or is it time to revise your dusty, ancient marketing strategy?

I can't answer that for you. But, what I can say is that, five years ago, I had this weird little idea that I could use my love for music and my appreciation for fashion, mix it with my desire to impact people's lives in a positive way and somehow infuse all of that into a tea business. I told my closest friends and family and they said I was weird. I looked at my 'non existent' credentials and completely absent qualifications, and even I thought I was weird. I skimmed through my bank account, and my balance whispered to me, "you're weird, not going to happen." Then I picked up a *'Where's Waldo'* book and tried to find Waldo. It took me a minute or two, but eventually I found him, and I realized that, Waldo's actually not weird. In fact, Waldo is not even hiding. Waldo is just wearing a different colour shirt and a hat and his glasses are really round. He was never hard to find, I was just always looking for someone that looked like everybody else. That was the problem. I decided to be who I really wanted to be, wear what I like to wear, and do things the way I like to do them; and now people are looking for me. It's cool, I kind of feel like I'm as weird as Waldo. Make any sense?

#BeSharp

#BeStylish

#BeMemorable

#BeDetermined

#BeSilly

#BeHeroic

PHOTO: HERMAN CUSTODIO OCT/12/13

#BeMagical

#BeDeering
(BadumPshh)

"The secret to succeeding in business,
is in the first two letters of business…"

#BU